This book is dedicated to all
Tanzania Tourist guides

ISBN: 9978-1-387-90052-7

The **Unique Behaviors** *of* **African Insects**

By Dickson Felix

TERMITES

(Isoptera)

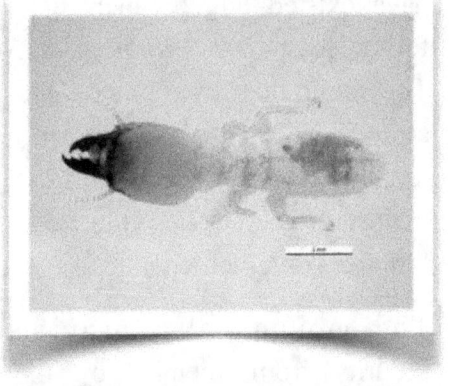

Although incorrectly thought to
be ants, termites belong to a
group of winged insects. There
are approximately 400 varied
species found in Africa. They
live extremely complex social
lives, even to the extent of

stretching outside their society deems relatively impossible.

Historically, termites appear to have existed largely unchanged for at least *100 million years*. They build their lives in a mound and these mounds function largely as a defensive fortress mainly protecting the vulnerable termites from their enemies.

The mounds also provide security from enemies by the way they are constructed in a seemingly air-conditioned atmosphere for its inhabitants. Inside the mounds, there are sterile workers who toil endlessly alongside the termite-soldiers.

In the reproduction of these termites, all males and females are produced by the female queen residing in the center of the nest with her king beside her. The queen "assigns" which termites will serve as *workers* and which ones will serve as *soldiers*. To distinguish worker termites from other termites, one must examine their color and size. *Worker termites* are pale or white, have rounded heads and bodies and straight antennae. They are smaller than the colony king and queen. *Soldier termites*, which defend the nest from ant attacks, also have pale or white bodies but possess dark heads and larger jaws. The workers are the ones who are in constant attendance to serve as workers and security advisors of sorts to the queen. The skin of these workers are formed from the queen's skin, using the process of exudation.

These soldiers have one major task; to defend the queen bee. Just as their name suggests, soldier termites are responsible for defending the colony. Soldier termites are bigger than worker termites, and they have a uniquely shaped, darker head with large pincers. They use these pincers to attack other pests that enter the colony, such as ants. They will bite humans if they are handled, but they do not typically seek out people to attack them.

The large, powerful jaws on the soldier termites make them great defenders for the colony, but they also make it impossible for the soldiers to feed themselves. They have to be fed by the worker termites, just like children.

Besides their large pincers, soldier termites have other options for defending the colony. In some species, soldier termites use their large heads to block tunnels that predators might use to enter the colony. In some species, soldier termites can emit a defensive secretion. These secretions can have a foul odor, or they can be sticky and poisonous.

Attention from the queen depends on the manner in which they have been groomed and fed. If it is to the queen's standard, they will be allowed inside the chambers. That is the reason not all termites are found in a queen's chambers.

On a typical evening, usually following heavy rains, a specific yet large number of termites are allowed out by the workers, After a brief flight, the females shade their wings and scurry about while raising the tip of their abdomens. The males become attracted to this process and after shedding their wings they run along in a tandem order. They soon stop and burrow themselves a centimeter or two below the surface to start a new colony.

They copy with woody society by themselves not able to digest woody directly is but some have culture of single celled organisms in their stomachs to digest food. Nourishment is gained when these organisms are digested themselves other termites such as macrotermes bellicosus cultivate fungus in chambers when fed on regurgitated wood pulp. The termites will eat the fungus which is already digested.

Harvester Termites

These termites do not form surface termitaria, but build network of tunnels below ground with many food storage chambers. Even deeper down, lie larger chambers sometimes spanning a foot in diameter, where the mobile king and queen produce their offspring. Periodically there is a nuptial flight similar to other termites species.

Dry grass provides the food of the harvester termites as a foraging by workers carries on the search for food by day, using their eyes; the only group of termites to have eyes.

CICADA

Insects with four membranous wings are held like a roof over their bodies. Ocelli are three jewel-like eyes situated between the two main, compound eyes of a cicada. It is believed that ocelli are used to detect light and darkness. Living on plant juices, cicadas produce a loud stridulate call. Only the males sing, the females are unable to produce sound, from the base of their abdomens. Just behind the hind legs are two semi-circular plates. If one of these is gently lifted with even the small point of a pin, a round shining plate can be seen at the back of the cavity. This shining plate serves as a mirror, and also acts as an ear. The females also have this shining plate cavity.

They have a timbel or drum not easily seen at one side of the cavity which is a tightly-stretched membrane with strong muscles attached. The action of these muscles vibrates the stretched membrane to produce the pulses of sound.

At the front of the mirror is a folded membrane which act as a sound board to increase the volume of sound. By raising or lowering the semicircular plate, cicadas can alter the volume output. This ventriloquially makes it extremely difficult for a would-be predator to locate the exact source of noise.

Cicadas can be found on groups of two or three, males and females, on a tree with their beaks sucking at plant tissue. The males will sing while the females lay eggs in slits in the bark of the trees. These reproduced eggs take weeks to hatch and when they are born, the young cicadas has enlarged front legs.

The newborn cicada falls to the ground and burrows down using their front legs. They stay below-ground during their entire immature life, feeding on the sap of roots. It is unknown how long they stay underground on the final stage, but when they do, they will barrow upward into the light and air, climbing a few inches up a nearby tree trunk to lie motionless for a while.

Their back skin splits and the adult cicada struggles free when its wings are dry. When their wings are completely dry, they will fly off to spend a few brief weeks in open-air singing monotonously. Some fully grown nymphs occupy a small subterranean chamber with a tin chimney protecting just above ground from which they break out when emerging as adult.

PRAYING MANTIS

(Empusa Gattula)

Carnivorous hunters use long front legs to seize and hold prey while rapidly nibbling away the edible parts as they fearlessly jostle insects as larger as themselves including spiders and bees.

The female will attack the male of the large species and has been known to bite off the head of the male during copulation. The female secretes a sticky silk-like liquid from her genital opening at the rear as she whips this into a foam with her hair, shaping it into an oblong form containing up to six small pockets.

She deposits her eggs nearly side-by-side in these individual compartments. The foam hardens on contact with air. After a month, the eggs hatch and small mantes are born, wingless and with their abdomens curled up over their backs.

Male mantis will moult antennae and are smaller and more slender than females. The males will moult several times before becoming winged adults.

The male have conspicuous feathery antennae and are more slender than the females.

STICK INSECT

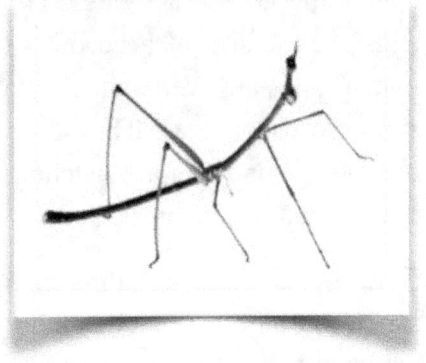

Very closely related to cockroaches and mantes. These are flightless and they remain largely motionless by day and move to feed by night. They are vegetarians and the male is usually smaller and more slightly than the female.

The female lays eggs in a casual manner producing them at the rate of one per day, while continuing normal activities. The eggs are the size of a head of a match and are very tiny, like small seeds or peas. They drop on the ground before hatching into immature stick insects.

The young insect goes through a series of laborious moults before adulthood. If a young stick insect loses a limb, another will grow at a subsequent molt. Males are rare and females sometimes produce without fertilization.

GROUND CRICKET:

(Kufamolongo in Swahili)

They are more related to grasshoppers than crickets; their reputation for being poisonous is unfounded. When handled, they squirt liquid from a hole on each side of the thorax, a place reputed to be a skin irritant and possibly makes the insect distasteful.

It bites with its strong growing jaws, and the armored, spiny shield on the thorax help make these creatures inedible to would-be predators. The female is recognized by her ovipositor, and the male has rudimentary wings with which he makes a rasping noise and the female only has ears just below her knees on her front legs.

Eggs are laid beneath the soil and are about a quarter inch long that hatch into small black kufamolongos. Since they are omnivores, they tend to eat virtually anything, including each other.

COMMON FIELD CRICKET

These characteristically possess long antennae, ears in their front legs and a stridulating organ on the wings of male. The female has a long ovipositor.

They are tireless chirrupers and practiced ventriloquists, making it difficult to locate them by sound. The rate of chirruping is related to temperature and it has been said that if the number of chirrups in 14 seconds is counted and the number 40 is added, that figure is within a degree or two of the air temperature in F.

Most are plant feeders but some household species can eat clothing. Field crickets are nocturnal and their formidable appearance is due to the development of their front legs burrowing. Some species of crickets live in trees and are small and have a rather anemic green color.

DESERT LOCUST HOPPER

The egg-laying occurs in December and January, and the eggs hatch in April and the locust matures, lives, and dies by the following January. At night the female forces her abdomen into

29

the soil and deposits up to 80 eggs per hole. She then seals the hole with a plug of foam secreted by her tail and then repeats this process in different places.

Two weeks later, having moved on with the swarm, three or four packages will thus be laid totaling about 200 eggs per female. Eggs take a month to hatch and then the small hoppers emerge and moult into brown insects with black and yellow markings.

Hoppers congregate and feed together mostly on grasses. They survive as wingless hoppers for between two and three months. Each of the six times they moult, their wings develop progressively. After the six moult, they are full sized adults with four strong wings.

If conditions are right these adults will swarm in masses over great distances. However, they don't breed in invaded areas.

ADULT RED LOCUST

These insects are famous for their catastrophic invasions, mentioned even in the Bible as the eighth plague. Locusts are divided in about 10,000 species grouped in 10 families. All plague locusts belong to the family Acrididae. The biblical locust was the Desert Locust (Schistocerca gregaria), which has been threatening agricultural production in Africa (Sahara and the arid area south of Sahara called Sahel), the Middle East and Asia up to India for centuries. For starting its invasions, this species needs a body temperature (depending on that of the environment) of 22-40' C. They are 7-8 cm (3 in) long; males weigh 2.2 grams while the females 3.5 grams. The females lay 100 eggs, and the larvae, wingless miniatures of the parents, get to the adult state in 15-20 days. The red locust (Nomadacris septemfasciata) causes severe invasions in southern and eastern Africa. Many countries in the northern Africa, Sahel and Middle East, like Yemen, Chad, Nigeria, and Mali, are extremely vulnerable to locust invasions. Locusts can jump 70 cm (2.3 ft).This is like humans jumping 18 m (60 ft)! Locusts and grasshoppers are closely related and have similar look and habits, that's why the question is: how can a person differentiate a locust from a grasshopper? Locusts have short antennae, grasshoppers have very long ones. Locusts "sing" by rubbing their rear feet from elytra (the outer tough pair of wings). Grasshoppers "sing" by rubbing the elytra between them. Locusts have short ovipositor (egg depositing organ) and ootheca (egg capsule); grasshoppers have long sword-like ovipositors.

SHIELD BUG

These insects have flattened bodies and can emit an unpleasant smell when molested, close inspection will always distinguish them from beetles because of the absence of biting jaws and their slander tabutat beak carried folded under the body.

These bugs feed on plant sap and some can be serious menace to crops such as Antestia variegate The Antestia bug is a menace to coffee stink bugs and they often appear in large numbers around lights soon after the breaking of rains. Some shield bugs will also prey on soft bodied insects such as caterpillars.

MAYFLY

These are very short-lived flying insects characterized by its usual two pairs of wings and two, sometimes three, long thin appendages on the abdomen. Mayflies are always found near water in the evening in graceful dancing swarms.

37

They usually appear after rain and they only live a few hours. The adults can't feed because its alimentary canal fills with air, which gives its buoyancy.

Mayfly swarms usually consist of males; the females join a swarm, pick up a partner and they drop out. In general, eggs are laid by the female dipping down slightly just touching the water's surface, leaving eggs as she does so.

In some species each egg has a bundle of finny threads attached, which support it and help anchor it to weeds. The females die as soon as egg-laying is over and an egg hatches into a larva which creep around the bottom of a stream keeping out of harm's way.

Feeding on rotting vegetables and animal matter, while going through a series of moults to grow, the mayflies are ready for adulthood. They now must pursue a hazardous journey to the water's surface avoiding hungry fish. Some species swim to the surface where their back skin splits and the winged insect struggles out and flies away in no more than a minute or two.

With other species the winged adult emerges below the water to generate a bubble of air around it in which it shoots to the surface and it's projected quickly into the air, dried. This winged adults are usually a dull, dowdy, creature (known as a dun by anglers). After a brief rest, a final moult color appears and the finished glistening stage emerges.

SPIDERS

Spiders have ability to spin silk and use this ability in an extraordinary variety of ways for shelter, dispersal and predation. They are ruthlessness when it comes to their predator behavior.

The widespread occurrence of poison and its toxicity of the use of silk mentioned can be made of four strategies:

(i)   Active traps;

 e.g. the net throwing spider (Din opus specie) which spin their web into a net for dropping onto passing ground-moving prey. Another use is holding the line of sticky silk taut which it releases to ensure prey collides with the line.

(ii)   Passive traps;

E.g. the large radical webs of the orb spiders (Araneus) which are used mainly to catch flying prey.

(iii)   Shelter traps;

Some species are using silk only to line their burrows e.g. the large palystes natalius, the trapdoor spider, combines burrowing with the trap, for it has a tough silken lid to its lined burrow which snaps shut when prey blunders down.

(iv)   Dispersal traps;

Many species of very small spiders and the young of others spin long threads of silk which cause them to be lifted off and dispersed onto currents of air.

The predatory habits of spiders hold a morbid fascination e.g.

jumping spiders use precision leaps (salticidae), spitting species use the sticky saliva missiles (scytodidae), another species uses its silk web more because of the ruthless behavior.

Some spider's species can survive months without eating. The venom of some species, in particular the button spider (Latrodectus species), is very potent but only minute amounts are injected at a time.

L.mactans, the black widow, is surprisingly wide spread over grassy areas of Africa, and its powerful neurotoxic venom is believed to cause about 5% human mortality in untreated cases.

The bite is very painful, other species in this genus are not as lethal but are still dangerous. Not all spiders are possessing neurotoxic, the genus Loxosceles has a powerful tissue poison that causes chronic blackish ulcers which sometimes require surgical treatment.

BABOON SPIDER

The king baboon spider, scientific name Pelinobius muticus, is a tarantula species native to East Africa. It is the only species in the genus Pelinobius. The king baboon spider can grow up to 20 cm in leg span.

FISH MONTH OR SILVER FISH

These are common, small, wingless insects that live in dark places and feed on paper and clothing. This can make them a destructive naissances.

They have poorly developed eyesight but a good sense of touch.

SOLIFUGE

Large spider like animals, they have a segmented abdomen and their well-developed pedipalps give them the appearance of having 10 legs. Their hunting strategy is to scurry rapidly over the ground tapping and probing with their pedipalps.

Their prey is taken by surprise during these random forays, and are held firmly by the pedipalps while being quickly demolished by the solifuges two pairs of powerful projecting jaws. Their bite is dirty and can easily become infected..

DRAGONFLIES AND DAMSEL FLIES

Adults are very beautiful and conspicuous winged insects. In dragonflies the hind wings are larger than the front pair, and at rest are held out stiffly from the body. Damsel flies have a pair of equally-sized wings which at rest are folded together above the body.

They are voracious carnivores, eating other insects, and their legs are stiff and structured so that they form a kind of "catching basket" in arrangement, Dragon and Damselflies can hardly walk.

Mating is an extraordinary characteristic, the male clops the female around the neck and the pair will fly together in tandem, the male always on front as they settle and the female bends her abdomen forward to reach the male's copulatory organ. Prior to this act, the male whose genital opening is in the tip of its tail will have bent his tail forward and injects a small dose of sperm cells into a special receptacle further forward on his body. It is to this that the female bends her abdomen.

It is a unique method of mating among insects, eggs are laid through the ovipositor of the female. This is armed by two pairs of sharp saws with which she makes small slits in plants overhanging the water. She deposits her eggs in each slit, and five or six eggs are laid in a row about 2mm apart.

Several such batches will be laid, eggs hatch into larvae which drop into the water and develop into nymphs up to 2mm long.

The nymph is an active underwater predator possessing a curious and unique extensible projection of its jaws with which it grabs its prey (known as the mask).

The full grown nymph creeps out of the water, up a reed of a plant and fixes itself firmly; the skin splits and the adults laboriously pull themselves out, creeping a little way up a stem leaving the empty husk below. It allows the expanded wings to harden for a while before flying away.

ANT LION

The adults have two pairs of
wings (transparent) well marked
with a network veins and are
often mistaken for Dragonflies.
They can be distinguished by
their antennae, an adult have
conspicuous, clubbed at the tip
whilst. The larvae are voracious

predators of other insects noticed scattered along sandy places.

When unwary prey walks over the side falling grains of sand alert the larvae which throws sand up the sides to hasten the preys slide to waiting jaws, the prey is sized, dragged bellow the sand and its body sucked dry through grooves in each jaw piece.

The empty carcass is then thrown clear of the pit, new pits are quickly dug by ant-lion moving backwards in a circle and flicking sand outwards with its head, and if one side seems like unprofitable the ant lion will move its trap overnight to a fresh spot. This is usually done by the insect burrowing along under the surface, the trails of these tiny creatures can be seen as raised ridges on the sand winding in all directions.

When matures the larvae buries itself two or three inches deep in sand and makes small chamber for itself within which it spins a spherical cocoon of silk and pupates, thus this pupa is small and it is astonishing that the long delicate winged adult can emerge from it.

The female lays eggs in a sheltered spot, the young larvae are often cannibalistic, eating one another if given a chance.

BAGWORMS

These are the group of moths in which the caterpillar spins a silken bag around itself to which are added fragments of vegetation which live inside. This exposes only the front part of its body as it moves in search of food. At the onset of unfavorable conditions the bag is firmly fixed to a twig closed over, and the caterpillar pupates are ready for the next rain season. The male is an active flier while the female is a flat maggot-like creature, quite unlike the male, she stays in the bag where she is mated.

WATER BEETLES

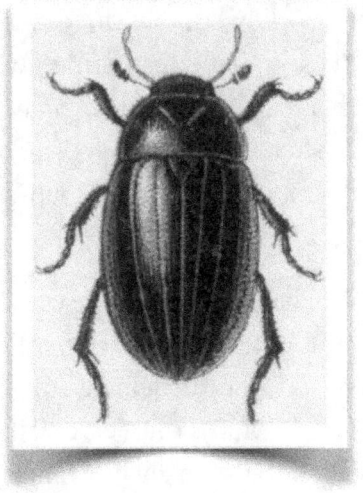

In general they are shiny and black with a yellow margin to their elytra and ranged in size from about 12-30mm.Most are active fliers and are attracted to the lights at night.

The hind legs are extraordinary well-adapted for swimming which they do with oar-like strokes called feathering with each return stroke. The body is flat, streamlined and so smooth as to be difficult to pick up and hold.

When handling these insects be careful of a protective spine they have on the underside of the thorax. Males have circular swollen pads on their front legs which have little suckers and glands giving off a sticky fluid which is the only way he can cling to the smooth slippery female when mating.

The female lays her eggs in slits in water plants, the larvae is carnivorous, grabbing its prey in its hypodermic jaws. Poison is injected through these which kills whereupon the prey is an air-breather and lives on air trapped between its elytra abdomen which it has to replenish occasionally.

TORTOISE BEETLES

These are leaf eaters often found in gardens and are conspicuous because of their brilliant metallic-colored bodies, Eggs are laid on leaves and are enclosed in a little blobs of hard transparent substances, sometimes distinguished by a small deposit of excreta on top. The larvae has an array of flattened branch spines on each side of the body and an obvious forked tail.

It makes a little chamber in the leaf in which it does not shed excreta nor old skin, but casts from various moults which become entangled on the forked tail. These moults become a black unsavercery gluey mass, as a defense in the face of enemies.

LONGHORN BEETLES

These are wood borers and include some of the largest insects measuring up to 100mm in length. They are characterized by their very long articulated antennae. They are attracted to the light at night and when they are handled they will squeak by

64

rubbing parts of their body together. Eggs are laid in cracks of wood and the hatched larvae are cannibalistic. A few remain after devouring each other, turning into the wood where they may live for up to four years.

Thuaelling larvae seem to be able to avoid each other as they bore through the wood and this is probably due to their vibration-sensitive organs on their bodies which alert them to the gnawing noises of neighboring larvae. The final stage hollows out a chamber and pupates. The adult has a nasty pair of biting jaws.

DUNG BEETLES

Dung beetles are sometimes known as Scarab Beetles. They are characterized by fanlike antennae which can be folded neatly away. The group is well represented in Africa, both sexes are very alike, and they seem to use their antennae to scent out the dung. However, these are well tucked away when beetles are at work. The shape, size and habitat are enormously varied, but in general they burrow their dung into the soil directly beneath the dung heap and roll balls of dung to transport them away to suitable ground. In the latter group, the dung beetle first breaks the dung pile using its front strong legs which incidentally lose their terminal segment, giving them more effective leverage and power. The best parts of the dung are gathered, patted, and pressed into a neat ball.

This is then rolled away with the beetle using its hind legs for the purpose of abiding it from the second insect who is probably, in fact, trying to steal it. The ball then buried a few inches below ground and a surrounding chamber excavated and the entrance tunnel blocked, the beetle then steadily eat the whole ball, taking several days to do so. After consumption, it will break off and fly away in search of fresh dung.

When the time comes for reproduction, the female forms the ball and transports it as before or sometimes buries it at a certain spot. The depth seems to vary with the beetle's size. She makes a large chamber and begins a long patting and smoothing process making the ball into a pair-like structure. She then leaves it, and it is covered-over making the ball into the pear-like structure. She then leaves the chamber closing the entrance behind her and flies off to repeat the process.

The eggs hatches into white larvae which eats the contents of the ball leaving only the outer shell. It then pupates and an adult emerges in due course, probably at the onset of the next rain.

There are variations on this theme, but the basic process is the same. For example, the bronze and green *onitis aygulus* digs a tunnel directly beneath the dung at the bottom of which a chamber is hollowed out and this is packed with dung in which eggs are laid as the dung packing proceeds.

Eggs hatch and the larvae live off this dung, each creating its own chamber separated from each other by only thin walls. They pupate and emerge as adults when external conditions are right.

"It must be self-evident how important dung beetles are in recycling nutrients particularly in semi-arid areas where fungal and bacterial decay is retarded due to dryness."

SOCIAL WASPS

These groups are so called hornets, to be found making their nest (papery nest) under verandah roofs, in shallow caves etc. A fertilized female starts making its nest by constructing a tough stalk. On this is built her first cell hanging with the opening downward. Other cells are added in concentric circles and she is then usually joined by other females.

Eggs are laid in the bottom of the cells at the halfway stage of construction and when the larvae hatch, they are fed by the adults with pellets of chewed caterpillar.

A very interesting feature of these social wasps is the behavior of the larvae which protrude from their heads with their mouths open waiting for foo. It has even been said that they scratch the sides of their cells to attract the attention of their nurses.

When touched, they exude a drop of clear sweet liquid which is much savored by the attending nurse who eagerly laps it up. It is also said that a nurse will ill-treat the larvae who does not produce her rewards quickly enough. The larvae's head is seized in the nurse's jaws, drawn half out of the cell and thumped back. This spurs the recalcitrant offender into producing the desired liquid.

When the larvae is fully grown, the cell is capped and the pupates of the emerging adults. The females stay to help with nesting. It appears older females devote their time to egg-laying whilst the younger ones hunt for food.

The males remain on the nest but do not work except to fertilize the females by which they are fed. When the nest reaches a certain size, a group of females leave to find a new one.

Other species of small social wasps, polistes species, build small nests from a single stalk. Alone female starts the nest and some of her offspring will be fully developed. Females, like herself and others, will be workers who will lay unfertilized eggs that develop into males.

MASON WASPS

These, together with social wasps, fold their wings longitudinally reducing the apparent wing width. This is a useful recognition character. They are also slender waisted,

75

and different species nest in holes in the ground or in steams while others build mud cells in sheltered places. An example of the latter is Eumenes caffer which is about 25mm long and marked with black on a yellow background.

The female constructs beautiful little honey-pot-like cells out of clay and saliva, and she lays her eggs inside this cell before bringing paralyzed caterpillars to it. This is usually how most mason wasps stock their nest with caterpillars before egg-laying.

The eggs of the E.Caffer is suspended by a thread in the middle of the cell, it has been suggested that this protects it from being damaged by the writings of the caterpillars within its reach and only dropping down when large enough to avoid being crushed.

The mouth of the cell is sealed over once it is stocked with caterpillars and for some obscure reason the carefully formed rim of the cell is broken down in doing so.

VELVET ANTS

These are smaller wasps of the *mutilidae* family, and the females are up to 12mm long and have a dark red thorax and black abdomen marked with white spots or bands. Males are larger and are winged. Females are

78

armed with a strong and painful sting and can stridulate by rubbing the joints between the thorax and abdomen together. It is said that if a female is held down while doing this, a male will appear.

All *matllid wasps* are parasitic of bees and other wasps. They seek out their nests probably by scent. Not a great deal is known about the life history but it seems that the eggs are laid in the nests to hatch and feed directly on the larvae of their hosts. The thorax is very, very hard.

SCOLID WASPS

These are solitary animals, usually black and marked with bands of yellow or red. Scolid wasps are known to be amongst the largest of wasps. The female is larger than the male, and a slight constriction is evident between their first and the second abdominal segments.

They prey as external parasites on the larvae of beetles. The female singles out a larvae, paralyzes it with her sting but does not kill it, and leaves it where it is while laying an egg on its underside. The egg hatches into a legless maggot which feeds on the caterpillar. Its cocoon is spun beside the shriveled skin of the exhausted beetle larvae.

SPIDER-HUNTING WASPS

These may be recognized by their long hind legs, curled antennae, and smoky colored wings. They run at great speed over the ground vibrating their

82

wings and antennae as they move in search of spiders. A good example is the large black pompilid wasp, or hemi pepsin capensis, which hunts the formidable baboon spiders and other large ground spiders.

The story of its hunting and nesting tactics is extraordinary by any standards and perhaps more so because as with all other wasps, it is instinctive. Its actions are a series of well-programmed moves hardly different from one hunting episode to another. Only the female hunts, and when she finds a suitable large prey she attacks fearlessly. Early accounts of the ensuing fight were that she stings the spider on the head to paralyze the fangs and then wrestles with it in order to sting it on its abdominal nerve centre. Her tactics are probably not always so precise and a sting almost anywhere will result in paralysis.

However, it is usually preceded by a short wrestle, the spider is only paralyzed and not killed outright. After a fight the wasp cleans herself and goes in search of a suitable hook for the large prey. Once chosen, she flies back to the paralyzed spider with an unerring sense of direction. The heavy prey is then dragged by her walking backward to the nesting site. If the distance is far, she will periodically fly to the nest as if to refresh her memory of its whereabouts. The spider is dragged into the site, an egg laid on its abdomen and the hole is filled in and levelled off and carefully disguised with twigs and leaves so that no trace can be seen at the surface. She then flies off to repeat the process.

The eggs hatch into a larvae which live off the spider. When fully grown, it spins a cocoon and when the weather is suitable, it pupates before finally emerging as an adult.

SAND WASPS

They vary in size from 18mm to over 25mm in length and have a black head, thorax and tip of the abdomen and slender rest waist. The females dig a hole about 50mm deep and their digging hollows out a small chamber at the bottom. Soil and sand are carried up between her head and front legs and swept away by vigorous kicks of her hind legs. Larger preys are dragged out in her jaws and she flies to drop them a foot or so away.

When the nest is dug she careens herself by means of the ting brush and comb on each front leg, and she sets off to hunt for the smooth caterpillars (cutworms) with which she will feed her offspring. Her struggle with these caterpillars is brief and fierce as she attempts to sting them on their underside causing paralysis.

The caterpillar is dragged back into the nest because it is too heavy to fly with, and she lays her eggs on it. She then emerges from the nest, fills in the entrance with sand until perfectly smooth and flies away to repeat the exercise. She will do this about a dozen times and then she will die. Some species will cover the top of the hole with a small flat stone before leaving and it is sometimes difficult not to credit these creatures with intelligence.

The egg hatches into a larvae which feed on caterpillar and when mature, will spin a cocoon and await the onset of favorable conditions, as it pupates before emerging as an adult. Some species are similar to the black and yellow mud wasp;

A sceliphron spirifex male makes its mud-nests beneath verandah roofs and suitable overhangs. These differ from mason wasps nests as they have elongated cells with the entrance at one end. Nests are usually stocked with small spiders. Half a dozen or more cells can be constructed in a bundle and the female will cover the whole structure with a thick coating of mud as extra protection. This complex behavior of these wasps is instinctive; for example, if spiders are removed from a cell and are brought without disturbing her in the process, she will bring her given quota. Although only one spider may finally remain in the cell, as if nothing had happened, she will behave as everything was in order. Likewise, if all the cells are removed just before she is due to do the final plastering, she will go through with this task despite the fact that there are no cells to plaster.

MATABELE ANTS

Ants are carnivores and most hunt termites. Female (queens and workers) have stingers, and as members of the colony, can distribute by rubbing parts of their abdomens together.

With the matabele ants, the workers are of two sizes; one large and one small. The larger one is slightly less than 12mm the larger, is black with fine yellow hairs on its body, and dull in contrast to the shiny small one. The queen is like the larger workers but with a stouter abdomen and the nest is underground with the entrance as a small hole.

They feed on termites making well organized raids to do so. When on a foray, they hatch in double-file and swarm into a termite's mound. There, each worker ant seizes a termite, maims it with its powerful jaws, and carries it to the surface. Each worker carries as big of a load as possible and all return to the nest. When molested, these ants give off a foul stink similar to stale tobacco juice.

SAFARI ANTS

These are known as driver or legionary ants that appear above the ground during the rainy weather. They can be seen as countless heads marching in dense columns. They are voracious and insatiable carnivores, the most common is the species Orylus helvolus, in which there are four types of workers ranging from 6mm down to less than 3mm. The largest have a powerful pair of jaws and appear to act in the defense of others. They are reddish brown and they are all completely blind.

They radiate from underground nests, sometimes spreading out into a uniform swarm, hunting for any living thing which they can overcome and tear to bits for carrying back to their nest. It is said that they occasionally move houses and have to carry everything with them including their young, the queen, and their pets such as guest beetles which are found in their nest.

The queen safari ants are extremely rare, so much so that only a dozen specimens have been described worldwide. She is a fat, brown, clumsy creature measuring at 30mm long. Her abdomen is swollen with eggs, making walking difficult. In view of her helpless nature it would be interesting to know how often she moves nests and what circumstances prompt these regular moves. It is also appears that she never flies, suggesting that she isn't a true queen but simply a specialized and overgrown worker.

The male safari ants is also interesting. He may be 25mm or more in length with a brown fluffy head and his thorax has a long brown abdomen giving him a nickname "sausage fly". He can wave this abdomen, although like all males this has no sting nor does he use his formidable looking jaws (in fact, he probably never eats). He is a noisy and ill-coordinated flier but can probably cover quite large distances. He has small eyes and is often attracted to lights at night. Blundering noisily about in a room, he probably flies

MYRMICINE ANTS

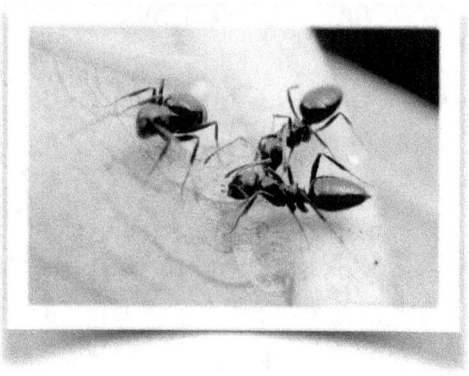

These show a great variety of habits and structures as the female can sting. Perhaps the most common is the brown house ant. Workers are less than 2mm long and the larger ones have a large square head around their powerful jaws which are not used defensively and probably are uses only to crush food and help with the heavier tastes.

Queens are dark reddish-brown and are 8mm long. Their nests are made in soil and their entrances are usually marked by small heaps of loose soil. They will eat almost anything but favor especially the honeydew of aphids, scale insects, and mealy bugs, which they visit but do not harm.

A closely allied group are the harvester ants which form large nests in the soil and feed mainly on grass seeds, the husks of which are deposited, forming a large mound. If the nest is opened up at the onset of the dry season, the heads of the large workers will be found piled in a chamber. It seems that they are slaughtered and eaten (except their heads) by other members of the colony after their main role of food- gathering during the rainy season is over.

The very interesting mymicine ants are the thief ants. The queen is a whopping 25mm long! While the workers burrow narrow tunnels through the mound, it is thought that the little thief ants creeps into the termite chambers and carry off eggs and young and once back in his narrow tunnel the larger termite cannot give chase.

An interesting feature of these ants is the need of the large queen to carry with her these tiny workers when founding a new colony. They are carried and caught up in dense tufts of hairs on her legs and so to travel with her. That is the reason for her need of small workers.

Another group within this sub-family is the cocktail ant. Their name is derived because of their habits of raising their abdomens over their backs and when alarmed, small white glands are exposed at the abdomen tip giving off a whitish fluid with an unpleasant odor. Others can squirt formic acid from their tails, causing stinging and irritation.

They are tree dwellers, with some species living in dead woods and others making so-called carton nests attached to branches. These are made of chewed vegetable fiber mixed with saliva.

The walls are thin and papery and the interior consists of irregular cells like a coarse but rigid sponge. The size may vary from that of an apple to that of a football. These ants, like sugar substances, will attend aphids, scale insects, and meal bugs etc, for their honeydew.

It is said that they will sometimes build small papery shelters over such insects to imprison them while they feed off their honeydew. The queen is generally bigger than the workers and the male is smaller.

FORMICINE ANTS

These cannot sting but they have poison glands which are used to squirt poison at an enemy. To do this an ant brings its abdomen between his legs and squirts forward. Some bite first and then squirt the poison on the wound.

Plagiolepsis custodiens is a South African species which attacks aggressively if its nest is disturbed.

They are brown and the workers vary in size, with the larger one being about 12mm long. Queens are larger still and darker. They nest in the ground and sometimes live in the walls of termite mounds and feed mainly on termites, but will attack almost any other smaller creature.

Some species of formicine ants have certain workers living in honey pots as they are forced to imbibe large quantities of nectar collected by other members of the colony. They become grossly distended by this and will regurgitate to colony members on demand. This appears to be the ant solution to the problem of not having storage chambers in their nests. An interesting member of this sub-family, common on the East African coast, is the tailor ant. This ant makes its nest between the leaves of trees which are held together by a fine web of silk.

The workers are yellowish-red in color and are viciously aggressive if molested, as they bite and squirt poison. Their methods of nest construction is fascinating; workers line up side-by-side along the edge of a leaf seizing the edge of a nearby leaf in their jaws and clinging to the former with their legs.

They pull in unison, drowning the two edges together. Now, as an adult insect cannot produce silk, other workers appear each carrying larva in its jaws and line the edge of the slit. They wave the larvae from side-to-side touching each edge with their (larval) mouths making the larvae thread together with the edge with the web of silk.

BEES

Besides the well-known honey bee, which is a highly social insect, there are stingless bees and a variety of solitary bees. In fact of the 10,000 species of bees known worldwide, only 500 are social.

The solitary bees dig a tunnel on the ground where they lay their eggs and the larvae and the adult develop. While the individual solitary bee works alone, the nests tend to be clustered together. Some bees show transitional stages such as the halictus species in which females work together digging a common burrow from which tunnels extend, leading to individual cells where each female will separately live.

An interesting species of bees is the group of the leaf-cutters megachile species. These are stoutly built bees with a conspicuous tuft of yellow hair on the underside of the abdomen which is probably for collecting pollens. The female seeks out a readymade hole, in a hollow stem, hole in a bank, hole in a tree trunk, or even a keyhole. Onto a base of this, she plasters oval sections of leaves beautifully cut from a neighboring plant. These are built up into a small cup-like structure.

A paste of pollen and honey is deposited, an egg is laid and the cup is closed with perfectly fitting circular piece of leaf. She then proceeds to make other cells and continues until the tube is nearly full.

Rough cut pieces of leaf are then stuffed into each entrance and a final plug of chewed leaf is cemented over. Carpenter bees are very large robust animals up to 18mm.

Mostly black with bands of yellow or white hairs, the female starts nesting at the onset of the rains. She actively bores into softish wood using her jaws. The wood must be dry as these bees are very susceptible to diseases caught from the fungi prevalent in damp wood. A consecutive series of chambers are then layered off with an egg and food supply deposited in each.

The remainder of the life cycle is not usual. However, a fascinating aspect of some of these carpenter bees is the occurrence on the body of the female of a small hole at the base of abdomen on the back. This leads to a larger chamber which will be found, carefully packed, and larger mites of a species are unique to these bees.

Their role in the life of the bees is obscure except it is known that they are always with the female. Occasionally, one or two will wander over the body to return again to the compartment, and those one or two bees will leave her body when she lays an egg and will reproduce alongside that egg so that the emergent adult bee will also have its attendant mites. Of the social bees, only brief mention will be made of the honey bee.

Only four species are generally recognized so far. The most common of which is the hive bee *Apis mellifica*. Many races of this bee are recognized and six are recorded from Africa. The two most important are the yellow banded race Apis *mellifica adonsoni*, which is the more common domesticated bee and *Apis mellifica* unicolor, a black form with a reputation of being vicious and difficult to control. Hybrids are known.

An important group of social bees are stingless, and they are widespread and common in the wetter woodlands of Africa. These are also known as moping bees, sweat bees, or eye bees and belong to the genus *trigona*.

Some are very small and they have an irritating habit of swarming and buzzing about one's face with a particular preference for nose, ears, eyes (and mouth too, if it is open). In short, they seem particularly interested in apertures or apparent apertures.

Some species can give a little nip (not a sting) as they nest in hollow structures and make a long spout or funnel to the entrance of their nest which is plagued temporarily at night.

PLANT BUGS

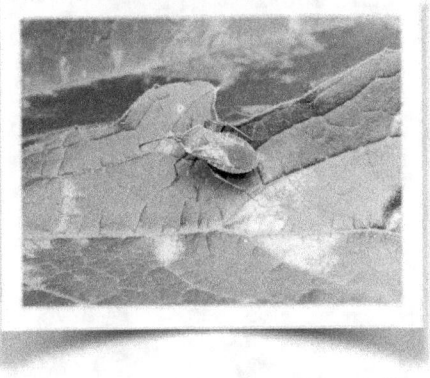

These belong to an order of insects called *hemiptera* whose central characteristic is mouth parts adapted purely for piercing and sucking. Some insects live entirely on liquids, either from the sap of plants or the blood of animals and cannot chew. They include stink-bugs, aphids, scale-insects, cicadas, bed-bugs, water boat-men, leaf-hoppers, and lantern-flies.

SHIELD BUGS AND STINK BUGS

These insects have flattened
bodies of characteristic shape.
They can all emit an unpleasant
smell when molested, and upon
close inspection will always
distinguish themselves from

117

beetles because of the absence of biting jaws and their slender tubular beak carried and folded under the body.

These bugs feed on plant sap and some can be a serious menace to crops. One of these species is the Antestia veregata. The antenstia bug is a menace to coffee, and stink bugs always appear in large numbers around lights soon after the breaking of rains. Some shield bugs will also prey on soft-bodied insects such as caterpillars.

ASSASSIN BUGS

These are vicious looking, often large bugs, recognized by their short powerful stabbing beak. Most feed on the blood of insects and other small animals or creatures. Some attack large animals including man, and one or two species feed on plant juices.

These bugs can inflict painful wounds and should be handled carefully. They lurk under logs, emerging at night. Some have front legs adopted for seizing prey and can be confused with a praying mantis, although the curved beak should readily identify them as an assassin bug. Very little is known about this group. Some are similar in size and have similar markings to certain ants amongst which they run and prey upon.

WATER-BOATMEN

Two families are recognized by whether they swim on their front or their back; those that swim on their backs have strong ridges but are longitudinally smooth like a bottom of a boat. They have overlapping hairs on the ventral surface with which they trap air for breathing underwater. They can leap from the common in shallow stagnant pools, actively preying on small creatures. They can make a chirping sound with their legs. The front swimmers are common in shallow pools with muddy bottoms and very little is known about them.

FROG-HOPPERS

These are also known as spit bugs due to the spit-like masses of foam on twigs and leaves in which the larvae lives. This larvae has a telescopic tail through which a watery excretion is manufactured and with which bubbles of air are introduced.

The full grown larvae leaves the form to moult into the adult froghopper which is a winged insect able to hop like a frog.

TREE-HOPPER

These are small bugs rarely more than ¼ in long, characterized by horn-like projections on the thorax. Ants stroke young treehoppers with their antennae and the tree-hoppers respond by exuding a sweet liquid which the ants enjoy.

LANTERN FLIES

Some members of the family have bright colored wings and could be mistaken for butterflies or moths, but their jointed beaks give them away. Certain species secrete waxy threads which they trail as they fly making them conspicuous in groups. The adults of other species occur in two or more different colors, and they have been seen to congregate. The whole mass resembles the flowers of a tree.

APHIDS

These insects are known also as plant lice because of the harm they do to many forms of cultivated plants. They are often seen in huge hoards on the tender parts of plants and they are harmful as they are carriers of certain virus diseases. They are also copious breeders, and the egg develops and hatches inside the adult female and is deposited as a young aphid.

As overcrowding becomes severe on a plant, some mechanisms ensure that young growing aphids can still develop wing buds and wings and are able to fly away. In warm climates these are all virgin births as there is no cross fertilization from male. Some ant species associate with aphids, running amongst them and tapping them with their feeders.

Aphids excrete by lifting their tails in response and exude a drop of clear liquid which is lapped up by the ants.

MEALY BUGS

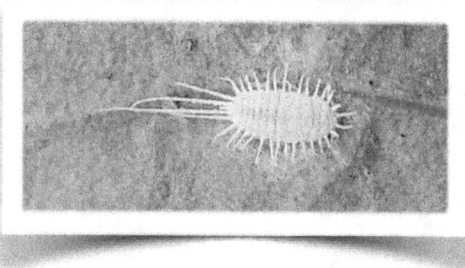

These bugs are smaller insects that are pets of cultivated plants that appear to be white in color because of the wax powder that covers their body. Eggs hatch into male and females which are tiny specks all alike. After the first moult, however, they change drastically and the female no longer resembles the male.

She continues to grow by way of a series of moults, while the male pupates in a cocoon to emerge after two or three weeks as a winged adult. He is a feeble insect whose only function is to mate and then die afterward. Some species like the cochineal are specific feeders on prickly pears and a species known as Dackylopius opuntiae has been introduced into Africa to perform this role. They have been quite effective together with other parasites of this problem-plant.

The ladybird is a voracious predator of mealy bugs and can provide a useful form of biological control. The female mealy bug produces a mass of fine waxen threads within which she lays her eggs.

LACEWINGS

These are related to ant lions and are pretty, delicate, green insects with golden eyes and very delicate wings. They are usually found on aphid infected plants, and they give off an unpleasant smell when handled, thus their nickname, the stink fly. The

larvae is active and armed with a
pair of sharp jaws.

Acknowledgments

I would like to thank the following people for their contribution, funding, materials, and support and advice of this book:

Jason Ratliff,

Bruce Cummings,

Sean Clark,

Nasser Al Azry,

Nehemia Daudi,

Nasser Al Said